A HARD LIFE IS NO ACCIDENT

A Story of Releasing

Victimhood and

Finding Oneself

MARSHA ARMSTRONG, MD

*I lovingly dedicate this book to my son and
daughter and to all on this journey called life.*

CONTENTS

INTRODUCTION—I Tried to Be Good 13

Feeling Misunderstood 17

Loneliness 21

Corporal Punishment 25

The Outsider 29

My Calling 35

Lack of Memory 39

Marriage 43

Waking Up 49

My Experiences with Men 53

My Past-Life Regression 57

My Continued Search 63

Energetic Downloads 67

Remembering the Trauma 71

I Wasn't Ready 77

2020 81

Releasing Trauma; Cutting the Cord 85

CONCLUSION—What I Have Learned 93

ADDENDUM 99

ACKNOWLEDGMENT 101

ABOUT THE AUTHOR 103

Every experience that I have had, perceived either as positive or negative, every person in my life, regardless of the duration of their time interacting with me, has been for my benefit or theirs.

MARSHA ARMSTRONG, MD

VICTIMHOOD:

the state of seeing one's life experiences as
hardships, mistreatments, unfair, or oppressive
circumstances.

MERRIAM-WEBSTER DICTIONARY

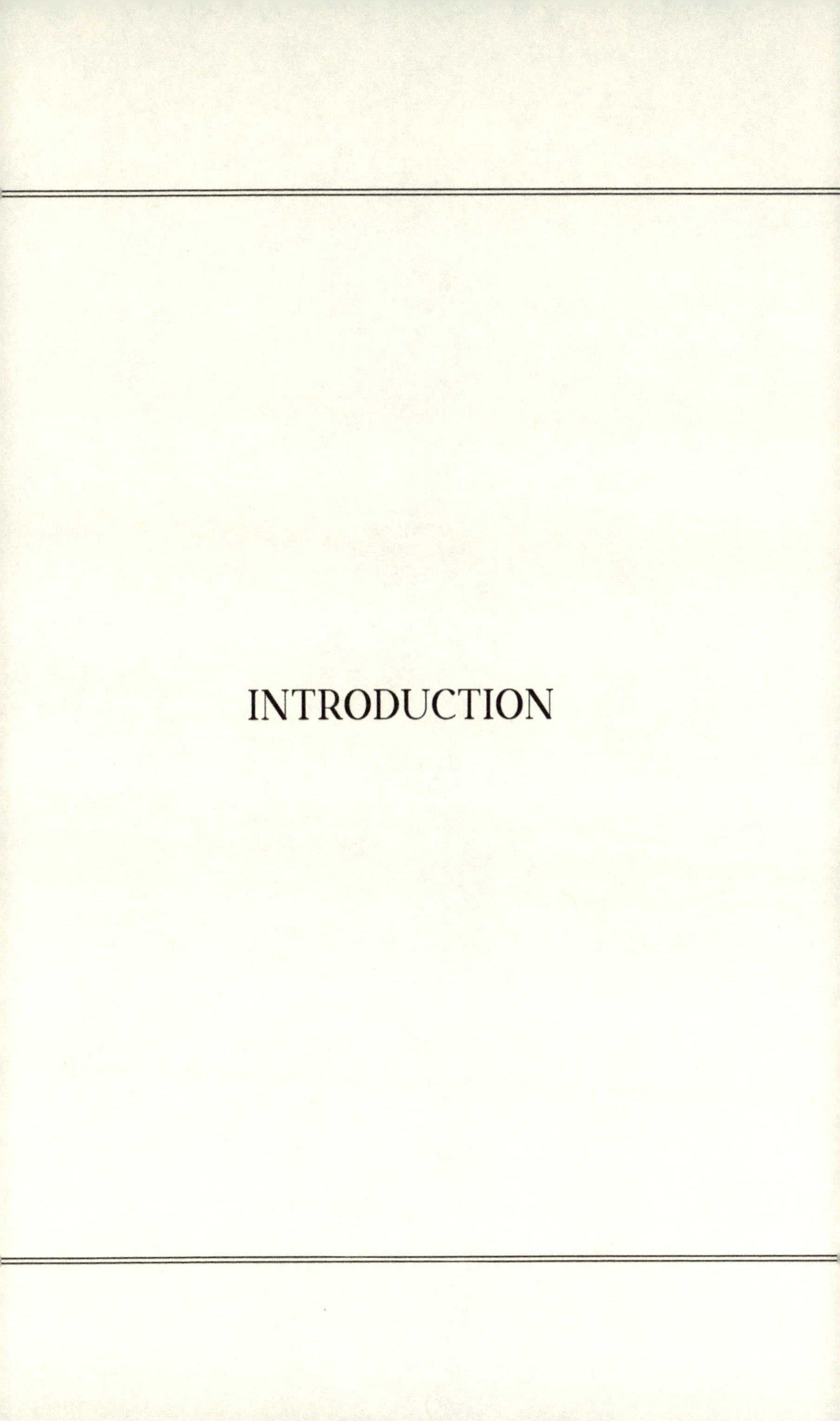

INTRODUCTION

I Tried
to Be Good

Why has my life been so hard? I have asked myself that question far too many times. Everything I wanted to achieve always came with a struggle. I compared my life with others who seemed to have the things they wanted handed to them. Or they were given guidance and advice that made the journey to their goals shorter and/or easier. For me, it seemed that for every step I took forward, I got pushed back two steps. Why was this happening to me? I knew there are people whose lives have been much more difficult than mine, but that didn't negate my experiences and my reactions to them. All my life, I tried to be good—following principles and ethics taught to me by family, the Catholic Church, and parochial schools. I was the stellar student, never doing anything wrong. I tried to prove I was worthy of understanding, respect, love, and acceptance—wanting to simply be seen and valued—yet life provided me with none of those things. *Why?*

I am an introvert, and keeping my thoughts to myself makes me feel comfortable and safe. However, I have been guided to share with you, somewhat reluctantly, my life's journey, one that has provided me with the answer to my question and the release of my victimhood.

Feeling
Misunderstood

When I was a child, people seemed to misinterpret my words, to misunderstand me. Around age ten or eleven, my family visited the home of one of my parents' friends whose family had much younger children than I. One of them had a toy kitchen set. I asked her what the appliances were to see if she could name them correctly. My father, overhearing my questions, interpreted them as my not knowing what a stove was. After we returned home that evening, he said I had embarrassed him. That was hurtful because I couldn't believe my father thought I was that ignorant. Much later, I realized he really didn't know me because he spent so much time away from the family while attending school and working full time. It wasn't until a little later that he realized I was a straight-A student and intelligent.

Loneliness

During my elementary and junior high school years, I had many experiences of being misunderstood and having to explain my statements to others. I began to think something was wrong with the way I thought and spoke, so it became easier to stay quiet, both at home and school, to avoid the embarrassment of anyone thinking I was unintelligent. Immersing myself in reading science fiction, watching *Star Trek*, and playing the piano and singing helped me to escape my reality.

When my mother started full-time work, my older sister and I became latchkey kids. We would come home after school, do our homework, and wait until my mother returned from work and prepared dinner. We would eat, then go to our rooms. My parents were aloof and non-engaging, and my sister treated me as if she wished I hadn't been born, as if she resented everything about me. When she *did* give me attention, it was only to grab one of the books I was reading and run away with it or say mean things to me like I was an alien. I didn't fit in at school or at home. Consequently, I spent a lot of time alone with my only true friend and protector, my dog, a German Shepherd named Geri.

As a kid, my life seemed normal. It was during my retirement, after having many energetic clearings, that I remembered how much loneliness and sadness from that time I had actually buried deep within my subconscious.

The summer before my freshman year in high school, my family moved from the inner city to the suburbs, becoming the first African-American family in the neighborhood. Rocks and debris were thrown onto our front lawn. My father spent several nights sitting in the foyer with a loaded shotgun. My parents kept those events away from my sister and me while we adjusted to our new environment. The isolation I felt within my immediate family was compounded by the neighborhood's distance from the inner city we had left behind, which was still home to extended family and schoolmates. We had to drive to see them. Also, the boyfriends of my sister and I were constantly stopped and questioned by local police when they traveled to and from our home. Eventually, things settled down, life continued, but my family never fit in with the neighbors. We were ignored, which, looking back, was not a bad thing from an historical perspective.

Corporal Punishment

My parents understood the importance of a good education and made sure that my sister and I attended the best schools they could afford: Catholic schools. My elementary school years, during the 1960s, were spent in an all African-American school taught by Caucasian nuns. Nuns who had no previous relationships of equal status with African Americans and who carried their own prejudices against those they were put in charge of teaching. Those years are a blur, but I do remember how cruel the nuns were in administering corporal punishment for the smallest infractions. It was all about conformity and discipline. If a small number of children misbehaved, the entire class was punished by having to stand in the aisles with arms outstretched at their sides for what seemed like an eternity. One nun had five wooden rulers held together by rubber bands, which she used to hit children over their knuckles for misbehaving. Boys got the worst of it. This practice seemed inhumane and unfair to me. How do you justify punishing the innocent, well-behaved student? Every class day, you had to worry that you would be subjected to this treatment, no matter how you behaved. There was always a level of stress and anxiety. This became normalized. School was not a safe, nurturing, or fair environment.

The Outsider

I entered high school in 1969 as one of nine African-American students integrating the all-girls, college prep Catholic high school class of 1973. There was a smaller number of African Americans in the three class years ahead of me, but integration had ramped up with my class. The other Black girls seemed to have known one another before starting high school, possibly due to attending the same elementary school or church. My sister was in the sophomore class, and though there were less than 100 students in each class year, I hardly saw her. Again, I was the outsider, feeling apart from the Black students in my class, and surrounded by White students (a new experience), most of whom really couldn't or didn't want to relate to Black students. Worried about being good enough—because the subtle and non-subtle messages I received from society said I wasn't— my main goal throughout high school was to prove I was just as intelligent and deserving as everyone else. I worked hard to get excellent grades; however, deep inside, I did not feel worthy, accepted, or seen in a positive light by anyone, even my parents. I don't remember them ever telling me they were proud of my hard work and accomplishments. I tried to be perfect—just to get acknowledgment or praise—but I was unsuccessful. This behavioral pattern continued for many decades.

The mid-1970s, my college years, were socially my best. I pledged into the first African- American sorority my first year at a state university. It offered social activities and the Black unity and support needed at the large white campus with fewer than 1,000 Black students. However, though African Americans were being admitted, by the end of my fourth year, it was quite clear that fewer of them were graduating. This, I believed, was due to poor preparation and academic support for most of those students in their predominantly Black inner-city school systems. They entered the university setting unaware of their disadvantage created by systemic racism. The university provided no real support. There was no shortage of faculty members and students who were not accepting the ethnic changes on campus.

I was a Biology major. By the time I entered sophomore-level classes, depending on the class, Black classmates were rare or nonexistent. I discovered that the White students had access to an abundance of old exams and study notes in each class. They formed close study groups for sharing those notes. I was never invited to join. There was also a lack of Black and Brown faculty members one could turn to for advice, guidance, or a sympathetic ear. I was aware of only one other Black student with a biology major who graduated from the university the same year I did. Fortunately, things have changed since that time. More minority faculty members were hired. Support groups and tutors were brought in, and copies of notes and old tests were being stored in the Black Student Union for all to have access to. Graduation rates improved.

On graduation day, my mother and sister attended the commencement ceremony. My father did not attend due to having back issues. I arrived home to find him sitting in his chair in the family room watching television, with a drink by his side. Though I was the second person in the family to graduate from college, second only to him, he offered no congratulatory statement, no pleasantries, not even a smile. My graduation seemed like no special occasion to him. It felt like he was not happy with my accomplishment. Confused and hurt by his response, I went to my room and watched television.

My Calling

After college came acceptance into medical school. Since age ten, I had known I was going to become a doctor, though I didn't really know why. My father, a pharmacist, wanted me to go into pharmacy because he thought medicine would be too difficult for a woman. He never said this to me but told this to my mother. Everything that was pushing me through school was so I would reach my destiny of becoming a doctor. The medical school curriculum was rigorous. I suffered from stress and a lack of sleep, but sheer determination and willpower got me through. Helping people with health issues was effortless. It felt natural and comfortable. It wasn't until I retired that I had a memory of being a well-respected and well-known healer in India in a previous lifetime.

In this book, I have deliberately avoided details about my medical career because they are not relevant. What is relevant is how my emotional and mental awareness and my spiritual growth during the past thirty-plus years have brought me to this point in my life. Toward the last years of my medical career, I became dissatisfied, disillusioned, and frustrated. I saw how the practice of medicine had and was changing. I began researching alternative healing modalities, such as acupuncture, homeopathy, and Chinese and Ayurvedic medicine. I incorporated herbal products into my daily routine and slowly eliminated pharmaceuticals in those few instances where I used them. My body became more intolerant of eating meat and fish, and I eliminated them from my diet. I was able to successfully treat my minor issues and maintain good health and a strong immune system.

Lack of Memory

As I have mentioned, I spent much of my earlier years feeling alone. At about age fifteen, I became bothered by the fact that I had few memories of my childhood before age ten. I had heard isolated stories from my family, but nothing like the childhood memories of my sister, who even remembered being potty trained! My lack of memory caused me to ask my parents, on more than one occasion, if something traumatic had happened to me that would prevent me from remembering. Their response was always *no*.

My curiosity peaked when I studied psychology in medical school. I questioned my parents again and received the same answer. Something deep inside said this wasn't true, but I was busy with school and life as a newlywed, so I pushed my questions deep within.

Marriage

I met my ex-husband during my first year of medical school while attending a conference for medical students. We dated long distance for one year. I then transferred to the medical school he was attending. Little did I know that my eighteen years of marriage would be the most difficult time of my life and would provide me with opportunities to have several life-changing experiences.

I had grown up in an era where the husband's role was to provide while the wife took care of the house and raised the children. However, like most African-American households, my mother worked full-time. I believe my father participated little in child rearing because he had two daughters and had no clue how to interact with us. By the time he wanted to spend time with me and my sister, we were in our mid- to late teens and did not want to spend time with our parents. My ex-husband had grown up in a household where his father had been the main breadwinner and his mother had, for the most part, stayed home to take care of the children. While I think he looked positively at the money I brought to the family, his attitude was that he called all the shots.

I gave birth to our first child at the beginning of my second year of residency and our second and last child was born almost three years later. To say this time of my life was highly stressful is an understatement. Having to study, be on call every fourth night with little or no sleep, then having to come home to take care of the children and everything else took a strong resolve.

During my first year of marriage, I noticed my ex-husband never asked my opinion or input on anything related to medicine, though we were taking the same classes and clinical rotations. I would ask him for input, so I thought that his not asking me in return was unusual. During the early years of marriage, I sensed he really didn't love or respect me. I pushed those feelings down because I didn't want to face their truth. I continued to play my role just like I saw my mother do. I was also aware that my ex still needed the attention of other women and was having extramarital affairs. He told me, quite frequently in the early years of marriage, that I didn't understand the concept of marriage and that my birth family was wrong in so many ways. He used "humor" to criticize and put me down, even in front of the children. I was the only one not laughing! I easily internalized and believed the putdowns during those years because I had already brought feelings of low self-esteem into the marriage. Those feelings had begun in my childhood when my critical parents hadn't acknowledged me or my accomplishments, even after I had tried to be a stellar child in every way. I behaved the opposite of my sister—never got into trouble, excelled in school, and was respectful.

Though my parents attended my medical school graduation, I don't remember them saying they were proud of me. My father did give me his *first* and *only* compliment, years later, when he told me he thought I was a good mother! I was shocked!

With my self-esteem at its lowest point, I believed every criticism my husband said about me, my sister, and my parents. I found myself pulling away from my family and isolating myself because I was ashamed of them. I was unhappy and frustrated.

During arguments with my husband, I was constantly told I was the problem. When I tried to discuss issues I had with his behavior, there was no hearing or addressing it. The subject of the conversation always loudly returned to me and what I wasn't doing correctly. I wasn't being heard, and what I needed to say was not valued! I became increasingly quiet to avoid conflict and criticism. I believed I was incapable of making any decision regarding my life. I could not even answer the question: *What do I want?* I lost my voice, my power, and myself!

Waking Up

I can't say one particular event started to turn me around. All I know is that I started to wake up. I now know that it was God's plan. I started to take my ex off the pedestal I had put him on and recognized his insecurities and the projections he had placed onto me. I began to slowly recognize myself, my strengths, and accomplishments, as well as my abilities. I became intolerant of my ex's behavior and found my voice. The more I found my voice, the greater and more frequent the arguments became. This self-awakening was a multi-year process, at the end of which neither of us was happy. Eventually, we obtained legal representation to start divorce proceedings. This was stopped early in the initial process because my children were having a difficult time with the impending separation. My husband and I tried to make things work. However, communication was non-existent. I became aware that my ex was having an extramarital affair with a woman I knew, whose children attended the same school as my own. I can't begin to express the anger and hurt I felt. I always believed that you end one relationship before starting another. I had to get my life in order because the divorce was on again as we tried to live under the same roof. This arrangement was mentally and emotionally stressful and came to an end when, due to a confrontational situation, he was asked to leave the house.

I was at my lowest point. I couldn't understand why everything in my life had been a struggle. I thought I was a good person, always trying to do the right thing. I was deep into those thoughts, crying so hard I could barely catch my breath; then suddenly, I stopped crying, and scenes from my life, starting at an early age up to that present moment, flashed before my eyes. I was shown how every event and experience had been a stepping stone to the next. Everything was connected and part of my life plan. By the grace of God, I was shown this, and I was profoundly changed by it.

Two years of divorce proceedings, my ex trying to break me on many levels, moving to another state for a better job, having my children placed in split custody, and continued issues with my ex until both children were in college took a toll on everyone, *especially* my children. I was once told by an elderly Italian psychic woman that the only purpose of my marriage was to produce my children. Initially, I had agreed with her assessment, but then I realized that finding myself, and all the other experiences from my marriage, had been vitally important and necessary.

Starting over after divorce meant taking one day at a time: some days being better than others. I did what needed to be done, took care of my daughter—who had decided to live with me while my son decided to live with his father—and worked at a new job in a new city where I knew no one. When I bought my first house as a single woman, I remember sitting in the living room the first night wondering if I could handle everything on my own. That thought and fear lasted only a brief moment because I knew I could and would. The self-confidence I regained during the latter years of marriage brought me to that realization.

My Experiences
with Men

The mental, emotional, and physical abuse I went through in my marriage was over, but the anger and pain from those experiences remained. I didn't return to dating until my daughter was a senior in high school. Even then, it was kept to a minimum for my daughter's protection. I entered my first relationship with high expectations because it was with a long-time friend from my high school days, but it was short-lived because I realized I had unresolved issues with my ex that I was taking out on him. My heart was very much shut down and I had a deeply buried distrust of men.

The second man I dated showed me a different side of male energy. He was a gentleman and considerate, it seemed. I allowed my heart to open up to him somewhat, only to have it broken when he unexpectedly broke up with me after he met and started dating another woman. Even though I was feeling unlovable, I tried the online dating platforms. I became frustrated with them but learned the various games, hustles, and lies perpetrated by the men on those sites.

A couple of years later, I met and dated a gentleman for about eighteen months, the longest relationship since my divorce. It was during this relationship that I realized I had a pattern of giving more than I was receiving. I was giving love, time, emotional support, energy, and money in the form of gifts and paying for entertainment. This was partially because my love language is giving, but I also realized there was a large component of my giving that was purely for the purpose of being liked or loved by others. This was a big *aha* moment because I also had this behavior with my mother. I constantly bought and did things for her hoping she would show gratitude and love me! Once I understood this pattern, I ended the eighteen-month relationship. I started to look within and became aware that all the men in my life, starting with my father, were emotionally unavailable, selfish, unfaithful, and untrustworthy, and that I was the common factor in all my relationships. I had chosen them! I had chosen those relationships so I could see what I needed to understand about myself. I learned much later that I needed to have compassion for myself and others, to have self-love, and that I was worthy of all the love and abundance waiting to enter my life.

My Past-Life Regression

My sister introduced me to books written by Brian Weiss, MD, on past lives and past-life regressions. I was unfamiliar with the subject but found it irresistibly fascinating. Later, I underwent a past-life regression in Arizona, during which I experienced two past lifetimes: one as a married Caucasian woman living in the 1800s and the other as a young Native-American man. As the woman, I saw my life during my early twenties, just married, and riding in a horse-drawn buggy to my new home. I was sitting next to my husband and could see the yellow dress and front-laced black shoes I was wearing. The home I moved into was in an urban area: a brick house with two stories. I remember the details of the home as if I had just seen it yesterday. There was a large kitchen at the rear that had a wide window that provided a full view of the backyard. All the dishes, cooking utensils, and pots and pans were neatly in place. A fairly large rectangular wooden table sat near the window. On the far side of the room was a staircase leading to the second floor. As I walked up those stairs during the regression, I saw a bedroom to the left. There was a multicolored, quilted spread on the bed and the room seemed heavy and felt somewhat dark. I had an instant knowing that I had died in that room after giving birth to a daughter.

The second past-life memory was directly related to my present life. I was a Native-American teenage boy. I had an older brother whom I adored and looked up to as a role model because our father had died. We lived with our mother in an area with open plains—mostly flat land with some low hills. My brother and I would spend time racing each other on our horses, riding bareback. We would laugh and tease each other. We had a special spot where we could look down and across the vast land. We would spend our time there just talking. During one of our trips there, we saw, in the distance, a row of covered wagons moving through what we considered our land. My brother became angry at the sight of this. We rode back to our village, and my brother put the horses away as I entered our mother's tipi. The three of us spent the evening laughing and talking.

The next day, my brother traveled without me. When he didn't return at the expected time, my mother sent me out to find him. I rode to all our frequent stopping places. As I approached the last location, I could see his horse from a short distance. As I approached, I saw him lying on the ground, face down. I jumped off my horse in horror, kneeled next to him, and turned his body over to see his face. He was not breathing, and blood had poured from a bullet wound on the left side of his upper abdomen. All the pain, grief, and anger I felt at that moment, I re-experienced fully during the regression. I cried uncontrollably with profound heartbreak. At that moment, I knew my brother back then was my sister in this current life. I needed confirmation of this after the regression, so I called my sister and asked her if she had a birthmark—a rounded shape on her abdomen in the left upper quadrant. We had never talked about having birthmarks before, but, to my surprise, she confirmed she did. After asking more detailed questions on the exact location, the birthmark was a confirmed match to the bullet hole location I had seen on my brother! My sister and I were amazed by the realization that we have experienced more than one lifetime together.

I had also been reading about psychic phenomena, a subject I really didn't understand and, at that time, had been afraid of. My sister had the ability to "know" about future events, a gift she had developed later in life. She would receive information about friends, coworkers, and strangers, but to my knowledge, not family. Also, during that time, books on various subjects that I had no previous knowledge of, just seemed to come to my awareness. I could walk through the aisles of a bookstore and certain books would stand out, attracting my attention. It felt like I was being guided to these books. Through my readings, I became aware of gurus of meditation, higher consciousness, and spirituality. One of those individuals was offering a guided tour of the Egyptian temples. I had a very strong desire to travel to Egypt. Not understanding why, I knew I needed to go. The group trip sounded perfect, so I signed up, made my reservations, and flew to Africa in November 2011, not knowing a single person accompanying me on the fourteen-day trip.

The first day, we went to the Giza Plateau and stood at the base of Khufu's pyramid, Egypt's largest pyramid. I stood there, taking in the activities around me and the people sitting on fallen pyramid stones. I felt this was not how I remembered this place from the past, even though I had not been there previously in this lifetime. I was saddened by the deterioration of the pyramids and how those now living there had no respect for or understanding of the place they were profiting from. They were not descendants of the ancient Egyptians, the original builders of the earliest temples and pyramids, but the descendants of the invaders who had most recently entered Egypt. I believe that is why they had no respect for the temples or the mummies of buried ancient Egyptians.

It was at the Temple of Hatshepsut at Deir el-Bahri that I either tapped into the energy of Hatshepsut or had a spontaneous past-life memory. While standing at the chained-off entrance to one of the rooms that went deeper into the complex, I began having vivid memories of being there in the past, when the temple was new. I could see the plants and trees in front of the central ramp. I saw myself as Hatshepsut standing in front of the second tier, holding a golden staff in my hand, my fingertips covered with gold caps, admiring the beauty of the temple and the garden in front of it. I then saw myself in a room surrounded by priests and other high officials who were standing around me as I was giving birth to my daughter. The lower half of my body was enclosed in a white cloth-covered, box-like structure that provided privacy. Those in the room with me were there to validate the birth. I felt their energy, that of disdain and anger, and I felt alone. I didn't know anything about Hatshepsut, other than she was a female pharaoh, prior to going to Egypt. When I returned home from my trip, I researched information on her and discovered she had had a daughter. This partially validated what I had experienced.

My Continued Search

The year 2012 was the beginning of my focused spiritual path that continues to this day. I became aware of a spiritual teacher who described God in a way I had never heard of before.

Information regarding who we really are beyond the physical, why we incarnate, and where our understanding and knowing of the self is leading us was presented. I started doing more direct and intense meditations and attended seminars where I experienced profound energy transmissions, shifts, and remembrances from this and past lifetimes that I had suppressed. I was beginning to learn to trust God and my life's path. This was not an easy task because I strongly resisted the feelings and emotions that were coming up, including that of anger toward God, an anger, I later realized, I had carried through many lifetimes.

Energetic
Downloads

On September 5, 2016, I had the first of three similar profound physical experiences. I was at home alone and had just completed a guided meditation when both of my hands started to tingle.

Becoming progressively stronger, the sensation moved up my arms. Both arms began to spontaneously and uncontrollably move up and down in front of my body. I was fully awake, alert, and completely shocked by what was happening. I didn't understand it and couldn't make sense of it from my medical training. The energy in my arms became stronger, moving to my shoulders and into my chest, which frightened me because I didn't know what would happen if the energy reached my heart. All I could do was experience it. I had no voluntary control of my body. After several more minutes of the vibratory energy in my chest and my arms still rhythmically moving in the air, the energy started to decrease. The muscles in my arms and shoulders were fatigued and my arms fell onto my lap. When the energy subsided, I heard the following sentence clearly: "You will be able to heal by laying hands upon."

It was as if someone was in the room with me saying this. I initially felt disbelief. I continued to sit in my chair, thinking, *Who can I call and share this experience with? Who would understand and explain to me what happened—that I am not going mad?* I knew of no such person at that time, so I kept the experience to myself.

In early February 2017, while attending another seminar, I began to feel strong energy moving through my body and hands. My arms began moving up and down uncontrollably, elevating to shoulder height. What happened in 2016 was happening again! My eyes were closed, but I saw a bright light in front of me. It moved closer, enveloped me, and I experienced an intense feeling of love. I then heard, again, that I would have the power to heal with my hands and that the power coming through them was from God. I then knew that this was part of what I had come here to do. I asked myself, *What do I do now?*

The year 2017 was one of continued awareness and change for me. As I continued to meditate and follow the guidance of a person who had high spiritual wisdom, I began to slowly understand the divinity within all of us and everything. I was being told to trust God, to trust in the unfolding of all aspects of life, and to surrender. It would be a multi-year journey before I was able to fully embrace these concepts.

Remembering
the Trauma

I began remembering bits and pieces of childhood events that led me to understand why I had little memory of the first ten years of my life. On April 7, 2017, after completing a meditation, I had a clear remembrance of an episode of molestation by my paternal grandmother's older brother. Later, in a conversation with my mother shortly before she transitioned, she told me he would come by the house frequently and unexpectedly while drunk. She had allowed him in the house even though she was uncomfortable with his flirting. He would somehow manage to be alone with me. I estimated that I was around four to six years old when the molestation first happened. He sat me on his lap with a tight grip around my waist. He unzipped his pants, then told me to grasp and rub his penis, showing me how as he held my hand. I didn't want to do this and tried to pull my hand away, but he grabbed it, forcing me to rub him. He then leaned his head back with a peculiar look on his face. I felt wetness on my hand and pulled my hand out of his pants. He let me go, and I ran to my bedroom as I wiped my hand on my clothes. I lay in my bed and remembered not feeling good about what had happened. I also had a knowing, after remembering this, that my grandmother had known about her brother's behavior but hadn't protected me because he had done the same thing to her when she was very young and was not protected. My mother was too weak to see the danger, and my father wasn't home that much because of school and work. As an adult, now remembering this, I couldn't help but ask, "Why me? Why did this happen to me?" As far as I know, my sister was spared from this trauma.

Memories of similar molestations from my father also came to light during meditation. Two of these occurred at around eleven or twelve years of age; however, most events seemed to have occurred before the age of six. One occurred late at night. I heard my bedroom door opening. My father walked in. He stood by my bed and told me to do to him what I had done to my great uncle. I was so angry after remembering those events. No one in my family had protected me! Sitting in my meditation chair, I damned everyone involved, yelling, "Damn you!"

Then, through closed, tearful eyes, my deceased father and great uncle were in front of me saying they were sorry. They, along with my transitioned paternal grandmother and sister, were standing behind my spirit guides, who were the buffer between us. I told them that I forgave them. I then asked God to forgive me for letting those events break me away from Him/Her, then I forgave myself. However, I was still carrying anger toward my mother for her role in these events. I was also aware that I had much anger toward her for another reason. She had never loved me the way I had wanted to be loved. Everything I had done as a child had been an attempt to please her, so she would show me affection. As an adult, I did things and bought her things for the same reason. I told her, in 2018, that I had memories of sexual molestation by my father and great uncle. The only thing she said to me was, "What did you do to cause it?"

I struggled with my hurt feelings and anger toward my mother for two years, until her last seven days of life. I was with her during those seven days in July 2020. Though she knew she would soon transition, when asked, she couldn't express why she had treated me the way she had, other than to say that I intimidated her. Eventually, I came to accept my mother and our relationship. I knew she didn't love herself, and so, she couldn't love me.

I had the type of mother I needed, not the type I wanted. The purpose of our relationship was to give me the opportunity to learn to love without the expectation of receiving love in return, and to understand the importance of self-love. With my father and great uncle, I learned compassion for generational trauma because I became aware, during meditation, that they had also been sexually abused as young children. My family lineage of sexual abuse, via our current soul-level agreement, was to end with me.

Additional awareness came to me in August 2023 about my parents. When my menstrual cycle started at age ten, my mother had my sister show me how to take care of myself. I didn't understand why she didn't instruct me. I became aware that she had my sister teach me how to wear pads and tampons because she could not deal with that part of me that my father had used and touched for his own gratification. She knew, very early on, that my father was inappropriately touching me. She even confronted him about it, only to be threatened (he physically and mentally abused her throughout their marriage) and told that it was none of her business, to leave him alone. I knew that, for some time, she couldn't understand why I could debate with him and disagree with him when she couldn't. That caused resentment on her part—toward me. I understood that she not only lost her power and voice when it came to my father, but in some way, she felt relieved that some of his sexual attention wasn't being directed toward her. She was so caught up in her own experiences and victimhood, she could not stand up for me or herself. Emotionally, she had nothing to give to me. My father was also immersed in his life's trauma and victimhood for which he had no outlet to resolve. He had lost his voice and power, which led to fear and rage, which he tried to suppress with overindulgence in alcohol. While having this new understanding of my parents, all I could feel was deep compassion for them. They had chosen a difficult life path and never gotten past their traumas to release the emotions and victimhood that held them hostage for their entire lives. I am grateful for my parents for providing me with the experiences I needed to develop self-love.

I Wasn't Ready

I retired from medicine after thirty-three years. I relocated to another state, thinking it was for a change and to have time to use the gift of healing I had been given. After I had settled into a new home, my mentor asked if I was just going to retire or start a business as a healer. I began working on my business, setting it up quickly. I attended several spiritual fairs and worked with many people; then, everything quickly ended. I closed the business. I knew it wasn't successful because it wasn't the right time. I wasn't ready! I had a lot more work to do on myself, including learning how to seek my own internal guidance.

2020

The early months of 2020 were no different than any other time for me, but I became more concerned as the pandemic narrative progressed. I watched news reports about the vast numbers of sick, hospitalized, and dying people. I listened carefully to what was being said, who was saying it, and how it was being delivered. As the year progressed, it became clear that things were not making sense. For example, all the opinions and statements being made by the medical professionals interviewed in the main media were the same. There was no disagreement or opposing opinion given. I had never witnessed anything like that in my career! It seemed that some information and medical definitions were no longer congruent with what I had learned in medical school. My intuition and medical training told not to trust what was being presented. I started to research related subjects, while looking for simple preventative treatment options. I felt a fear-based urgency to share my information with friends and family. To my surprise, what I said fell, for the most part, on deaf ears, or I was called a conspiracy theorist. I felt the fear-mongering propaganda had taken away the logical minds of those I'd wanted to protect. I became angry, frustrated, and concerned for those who believed everything being told to them by the "authorities." This put me in a state of fear—a low, vibrational energy. I had to release it! So, I spent much time in reflection and meditation. I had to realize that those I was trying to influence had their own divine path in life, one I could not control or change. Accepting that brought peace and compassion. As the pandemic narrative played out, the things I knew and was saying were eventually shown to be correct.

Releasing Trauma;
Cutting the Cord

Over the next two years, I continued my meditations and the energetic clearing of old emotions, many of which I thought I had already released, especially fear. I became aware of more fear from my childhood, fear of both my parents, as well as fear from past lives that were deeply rooted in my unconscious memory. I became aware of my continued anger at God for allowing the trauma, torture, and death to happen to me in my past lives, as well as for my experiences in this life. I had a knowing that I had lived many past lives where I had been the keeper and guardian of ancient knowledge. Because I would not release this knowledge to malevolent individuals, I was tortured and/or killed. In one of my past lives, each of my legs was tied to a different horse. The horses were made to run in opposite directions, causing my legs to be pulled from my body. The trauma from those lifetimes was still within me in this lifetime. It manifested as my being afraid to use my voice, to share my divine gift of healing, and to let my light shine for fear of being seen and silenced again.

As mentioned earlier, all the men in my life were emotionally unavailable, selfish, unfaithful, and untrustworthy. Having become aware of that pattern, I changed myself and stopped bringing those types of men into my life. However, I failed to fully understand the reasons for those interactions. That understanding came to me near the end of 2022. I realized I had put the men in my life on a pedestal because of a deep, unconscious belief that they were superior to me. I also chose them in this lifetime to help remind me of a platonic, teacher-student relationship I had had repeatedly over many past lifetimes and had been in this lifetime.

As I remembered some of the past lives in which I had either been shamed, tortured, or burned alive, it seemed that this person had been there. I had a knowing that this individual was aware of the knowledge and energy I carried in those past lifetimes and wanted it. Therefore, I was reported to the authorities, witch-hunters, or was otherwise silenced and suppressed by the influence of this person. In this lifetime, this person was one of my mentors. As I had done many times before, I put this person on a high pedestal and handed over my power.

I had many profound awarenesses and spiritual awakenings during this time, for which I am grateful. But, as I came to know my true self, I felt there was nothing more this person could offer me, and I started to pull away. I saw his humanity, his divinity, and his imperfections. The pedestal started to crumble. My higher self gave me the knowing that he had slowed down my spiritual progress at one point in this lifetime so he could hold on to the power I had given him. He had been aware, and I was not, of the level of divine energy that was to come through me into the world. I felt that he was envious on his human level, not fully accepting why it wasn't for him. As was the case in many past lifetimes, this was the final playout of this multi-lifetime experience, and part of the perfect plan for my life. I had, unconsciously and consciously, participated in that experience, having created a soul-to-soul agreement with this person so I would wake up and know myself as the divine being that I am. I was not a victim in this experience, and I can only be grateful for the role he played in my evolution.

Seeking guidance from my higher self, I asked what I could do to prevent this from happening again. I was told to reclaim my power, to be resolved that I had come here for a purpose, that I would not be stopped, and that this is the time I must allow what needs to flow through me into the world because the world is now ready for it. I was told to stay confident and to always remember who I *am*. I was told to love and trust myself, and that those supporting me are always with me.

October 20, 2022, was the day I visualized the energetic cord I knew was connecting me to my mentor . Having misinterpreted the meaning of that cord for many years, I visualized cutting it. As soon as that was done, I experienced a tremendous amount of energy entering my body in the region of my heart. The force of this returning energy was so strong it felt like I was being pushed into the back of the chair I was sitting in. I was unable to move for several seconds. I knew then that I had taken back my power and that it would never be given away again.

# CONCLUSION

What I Have Learned

Life is not only about seeing value in the good times—I had to learn this. We often pray for the easy way, for good health, loving relationships, the best job, a reliable car, more money, etc. Do we ever expect or ask for the challenge, the difficult relationship, the departure of a loved one, sickness, an abusive marriage, for any difficult situation? Why not? I believe we have been conditioned to only want what we call "good" experiences in life. In some cases, we feel we must have done something to deserve the "bad" experiences. We believe that if we do everything by the book, we shouldn't suffer. Where did that come from?

We came here to experience and to grow. It is through life's challenges and difficulties that we learn the most. Maybe, a challenge forces us to tap into our never-discovered creative side to solve a problem. Or maybe going through an abusive relationship is giving us the opportunity to love ourselves enough to get out. Or maybe repetitively selecting the wrong people to be in relationship with gives us insight into what we feel is deficient within ourselves: self-love. Maybe, the life-threatening illness gives us the opportunity to view life differently or learn not to fear death. Or, not having loving parents gives us the opportunity to look within for the greatest source of love there is. Or maybe the fearful, angry or difficult person is in our life to give us the opportunity to respond differently, to respond from a place of love and not fear or hurt. Or maybe our struggle helps us to have compassion for others or to develop resiliency. What can be particularly difficult is seeing aspects or behaviors in ourselves that we reject or disapprove of in others.

What helps me is the understanding that I chose my experiences before incarnating into this and prior lifetimes. Those who played a role in my past lives and my current life had a soul agreement *with me* to interact with me in ways that provided the experiences I wanted and needed to remember who I really am. Every experience—perceived either as positive or negative—every person in my life, regardless of the duration of their time interacting with me, has been for my benefit or theirs. This is true for everyone. Today, because of this remembrance, I no longer have anger or resentment toward any family member, past relationship, coworker, mentor, acquaintance, or stranger. They all played their part in my remembering and being who I am, and I am deeply grateful.

I am a divine, eternal being experiencing life through my physical body, which was created specifically for this lifetime. This is true for all of us. I have experienced my true self as part of and at one with everything—as part of God, infinite, expansive, limitless, as love and light! I now understand that everything and everyone is connected as individual expressions of God-consciousness, which dwells inside each of us as our souls. Therefore, we are connected to, and have never been separated from God.

The most difficult part of my journey has been learning to trust God's plan for my life and knowing and accepting that everything is unfolding in divine order. When I review my life up until now, I can see the perfection of everything that has happened. I can see it in the pain, struggles, and tough experiences I thought I shouldn't have to go through. I also see it in those moments of peace and joy.

I lived most of my life in victimhood, asking, "Why are bad and difficult things happening to me?" That victimhood, mental bondage, caused me to feel sorry for myself, to hold resentments, fear and anger. More importantly, victimhood caused me to lose my voice, give away my power, and feel unworthy. It prevented me from remembering who I am. I now understand that I am not, nor have I ever been, a victim! None of us are. Release of the mental bondage allowed me to understand that life is a journey to *love*—the journey to remember, while in physical form, that love, which is God, is in all of us and unites us as one.

We are born into this world without memory of who we are: divine beings, parts of God. We play along with our pre-birth script so that someday we will lose the amnesia and remember who we really are, and in so doing, stop giving our power away to others and start creating our own narrative, which is based on knowing the love and light that we are. When we create our experience from love, darkness is replaced by light, and we create *Heaven on Earth*!

ADDENDUM

My journey continues. Throughout 2023, I continued to have spontaneous energy clearings and new understandings. I continued to release elements of fear and doubt. I had to release the fear and doubt of not being able to fully express myself as my true self. I had to release my fear associated with telling the world my story through writing this book. I had to release the fear of what family, friends, and previous colleagues would think of me. I also released the egoic attachment of being concerned that no one would read this book. I came to realize that those who are meant to read it will read it and get out of it what they need.

My third energetic download regarding the healing that would come through my hands occurred on the evening of October 4, 2023. The events were identical to the other two experiences and confirmed that helping others through healing is what I am to do next. I am now ready! I know that this healing energy is from God. It is healing of the physical, mental, and spiritual. Each person will receive the level of healing that is meant for them. It is not my choice. I am only the conduit through which it comes.

ACKNOWLEDGMENT

I am eternally grateful for God's love and for all the beautiful souls in my life that are currently embodied, as well as those in spirit, for their part in assisting me in my life's journey. My love to all.

To my daughter and my dear friend, Mary Ann Morelion, thank you for your continuous encouragement and support and for wisdom given on the review of my first draft and title selections. Love you always!

ABOUT THE AUTHOR

Marsha Armstrong, MD, is a retired board-certified physician.
She can be reached at: www.marshaarmstrongmd.com.

www.ingramcontent.com/pod-product-compliance
Lightning Source LLC
Chambersburg PA
CBHW062234150726
47991CB00006B/2576